ALSO BY NOAH ELI GORDON

Is That the S

Coming from Severa

Noah Eli Gordon

*Is That the Sound
of a Piano
Coming from
Several Houses
Down?*

SOLID OBJECTS
NEW YORK

Printed in the United States of America

Design by HR Hegnauer

ISBN: 978-0-9862355-7-3

Library of Congress Control Number: 2017959309

SOLID OBJECTS
P.O. Box 296
New York, NY 10113

The Problem

A woman accidentally walks into the men's room. A man deliberately walks into the women's room. I don't believe in dialectics but abide by them nonetheless. It is like a painting of someone sheathing a sword. The problem is it is also like a painting of someone unsheathing a sword.

The Problem

Here, I want to describe in exact and blinding detail the particulars of three pigeons landing on a neighbor's roof. Here, I want to perfect the appearance of an indifferent and aloof countenance. The problem is not that both desires appear at once, but that both desires appear at once awkwardly indistinguishable.

The Problem

If he sleeps with the windows open, the noise of morning traffic wakes him several hours too early. If he sleeps with the windows closed, the heat of the stuffy apartment makes for a restless and difficult night. Between these two options, as between the unconditional love of two exemplary and devoted parents, the problem sleeps like a baby.

The Problem

She writes a stunningly accurate review praising the reclusive novelist's long-awaited new book. Upon its publication, a key sentence of the review contains an error of omission that, while minor, reverses her intended meaning, rendering the piece as a damning take on the book. Still, there is near-universal agreement as to her review's stunning accuracy. The problem is, as any good narrator knows, accuracy is never stunning.

Tiny Love Poem

When you pick up
one of the guitars

I want to pick up
the other guitar

The Problem

I walk into the arid desert. There are so many ways to begin. For example, as though unsure of the instruments, a fly bungles its liftoff from the windowsill's thicket of dust. I walk into the desert as into an idea of deserts. This, too, is a beginning. A girl pointing toward an ostrich insists that it's something else. "That ain't real," she repeats twice to an adult looking elsewhere. Our fly rounds the surface of an orange on the kitchen counter. An idea, too, has a surface, a skin. Of course it's hot out here. Upon closer inspection, there are streaks of greenish-yellow on the orange's corrugated exterior. An ostrich does not bury its head in the sand; it lays its neck flat to the ground so as to appear from a distance like a mound of earth. That facts are innumerable is not the problem. That we tend to look elsewhere is.

The Problem

In order to retrieve the password one must enter a user-
name which is itself retrievable only with a password. I've
forgotten which day to place the recycling curbside. Bear
with me; this is relevant. If I get the day wrong, a park-
ing space is wasted, irritating the neighbors. If the bin
fills, they're also liable to become irritated. The problem
is when something is liable to happen it is likely to do so.
In this way, I draw a beautifully exact circle.

The Problem

Someone tied to a parking meter the dog that barks every time a woman approaches to insert a quarter. This makes her the subject. It is a metaphor for the aristocracy of money. One performer plays both leash and dog. Another stands in for the meter. I play the woman. Someone appears offstage. It is often difficult to tell a king from a queen. The problem is no one plays the difficulty.

The Problem

He starts with 16 apples. She starts with 64 apples. If he gives her two of his apples for every eight that she has, how many … wait … math is for some a beautiful art. Within the movement and manipulation of digits they see an enormous mass of sunlight assemble itself into an exceedingly clear day. The problem is I just see apples, thousands of them.

The Problem

Just as she stops her run to smell the night-blooming jasmine, a woman across the street shouts: *Stop, Jasmine, stop*—not at her, it turns out, but at the child she didn't notice, the one standing there plucking trumpet flowers and tossing them at her feet. Listen, this is a true story. You can either eat this marshmallow now or wait fifteen minutes and I'll give you two. Once an experiment becomes famous, it's no longer an experiment. The problem is you can't lounge in obscurity, you can only languish.

To My Contemporaries

We crawled
out
of the
same body
of water

But somehow
emerged
on
different
shores

The Problem

He has in the middle of an important phone call an over-whelming need to urinate and fills the toilet bowl with paper towels in order to dampen the sound. This is the opposite of finding your voice. Played in reverse, it resembles a postcard of a beautiful sunset stuffed haphazardly into the mailbox. The problem is it's the wrong mailbox.

The Problem

The first person the social networking website suggests you befriend is the one most responsible for your obsessive compulsion to check for friend suggestions. This is the problem with the first person: the first person is too selfish; the second person, too accusatory; the third person—just plain distant. It's like a train whistle without a train, this barbaric act of writing poetry after the internet.

The Problem

He feels a strange, superficial obligation to say hello to his neighbor when they cross paths on the porch, pass on the stairway, stand, amazingly, at the front door together, keys awkwardly in hand, walk by each other in the back alley, exiting the laundry room, taking out the trash, picking up the mail, anywhere, really, just on the periphery of public space, in those transitional places between the private security of one's apartment and all the exits and entryways it abuts, all the blurred edges around what constitutes being at home, but never, no matter what, and herein lies the problem, never when they're both out on their respective balconies, even though only a slight partition—a two-foot tall railing really—separates them, even though they could almost touch, almost be page turners for the symphonic quiet of the personal space they're both intent on maintaining. But maybe I'm wrong; maybe it isn't a problem at all. Maybe they've exchanged pleasantries on numerous occasions, even become fast friends, sharing chitchat and dinners, commiserating, drinking, eventually moving in with each other as lovers. I couldn't say for sure. I say hello when I have to, but only in passing, only outside, near the front door, or the steps, but never out here, out on the balcony, where the treetops are so close, so goldenly comforting.

The Problem

The video she wants to watch takes an exorbitantly long time to load, so she opens a new window to watch a different video while waiting, which also takes an exorbitantly long time to load, so she opens a new window to watch a different video while waiting. As though stuck forever between Dante and Beatrice, sometimes the problem is this transparent.

The Human Face Projected Anywhere but on Another Human Face

A dandelion

smeared

across concrete

takes the shape

of its assimilation

in stride

The Problem

This key opens that lock, while that key opens this lock. A camera pans from one to the other. They are not related, and therefore have no visitation rights. The problem is not a literary device. It's the divisiveness of literature.

The Problem

She writes a pamphlet railing against the use of the word *project* to accurately describe the work of the poet. He writes a book railing against the use of the novel to accurately render the reality of our lives as we experience them. The polemic is in love with accuracy. The problem is it's the enemy of art.

The Problem

She likes how she looks from the side in the dress she forgot at the beachfront motel, from the back in the skirt lost at the seaside resort, and the front in the blouse she left in the back of her ex-boyfriend's new car. That's it really. The story doesn't have to move anywhere. I look at the sunset from my porch and you look at the sunset from your porch and the sunset and the porch and the both of us are irrelevant. The problem is the looking.

The Problem

Although the airport smoking lounge has a one drink minimum, he figures it's busy enough that he'll get in at least half a cigarette before the bartender takes his order. To make him a nonsmoker would be one way to explicate the problem. Look at how beautifully this tall grass sways in the wind. Doesn't it resemble a green surf? Can't you almost hear the seabirds and sad rumble of that tugboat's horn? Obviously, the problem is the order.

The Problem

A man has a novel idea. A woman has an idea for a novel. It's astonishing to deny the centrality of any single theme. First you have it, then you don't. For example, take the man and the woman. Introduce them to one another. Subtract the novel. In this way, the problem works itself out perfectly.

The Problem

The CEO of a major company has never used the product for which his company is most well known. Every morning, he irons his own shirt. He doesn't do this with the satisfaction of having saved what little money a dry cleaning service would have cost him; he does this because he enjoys the weight of the iron in his hand. The problem is not that it's the wrong iron, but that he's never heard the sad rumble of a tugboat's horn.

An Inky Piece

of vagueness painting a bird

Something

in its orange beak

Orange something

The Problem

I can't figure out how to explain that narrative is the order in which one marshals in the elements of a story without writing a story. For example: High up in the canopy of an elm, a squirrel takes stock of its winter supplies. Or: A squirrel examines food stored in the upper limb of an elm. In both cases, all of the elements are in order. The story begins with the anxiety that assembles them this way. It's the explanation that's the problem.

The Problem

His latest project is a long poem composed of several thousand similes without subjects. Like golf. Like a taxidermist manipulating the skin of a marmot. Like a child's drawing of a treasure chest tossed into a creek. Like the moon mentioned seven times in a run-on sentence. Like the problem.

The Problem

She suddenly remembers having long ago gotten rid of those terrible books by the author she's reluctantly putting up next week and so spends the afternoon going from bookstore to bookstore in the hopes of replenishing the shelves he's sure to scour, eventually buying back the very copies he'd inscribed to her so many years ago, and thusly avoiding the problem altogether.

The Problem

I go to the fiery lake to eat words of power. I interview a poet who expresses disdain for those who write things they clearly do not believe. I believe the problem is paratactic. From now on, f-i-e-r-y will be spelled f-i-r-e-y.

The Problem

She finds to be charmingly charismatic a man who has said awful things about her, things she's heard from a mutual friend, and so begins to avoid him whenever possible. To tell the truth is one tenet of fiction. This is part of its charm. One can fashion a necklace out of it but rarely find a blouse to match. I'm pretty sure their mutual friend is the problem.

The Problem

He sends a hurried email to a distant relative detailing the particulars of his upcoming arrival—dates, places, a somewhat transparently formal tone, and immediately regrets not having done so in a more intimate fashion, with a postcard perhaps. Perhaps with this one, the one where the sun is either rising or setting, flanked by high clouds and flecked with pink, like the meat of a flower whose name he's failed to learn. It's as though he's realized there was music playing because there isn't anymore—the sudden silence of the world as much an indescribable flower as it is the description of one staring directly at it. The sun, rising and setting, setting and rising. But not, as we know, in that exact order.

The Problem

My landlord installs a new banister on the front porch which from this chair obstructs my view of the faces of those who pass. My wife, it turns out, dislikes aphorisms, although I've written one for her: ethics is always a voyeuristic endeavor. The people pass, but they're no longer "the people." When I say dislikes, I mean vehemently, but I'm not even talking here. It's like a birdsong to a bird. The problem is purely evaluative.

Perfect Gears of Industry like an Alligator Lay in Wait Exhaling Evaporating

Vibratory machinery, grainy
octagons, ambiguously
the photons wend.
All nature poems want
to repeat themselves.
Vibratory machinery, grainy
machinery.

The Problem

A man commits to a hat for the evening, and the problem is sentience. A hat commits to a man for the evening, and the problem is absurdity. Remove the hat, and the man's commitment goes bananas. Remove the man, turn the hat upside-down, and place the bananas inside of it. There, now that looks nice.

The Problem

She avoids at all costs the use of escalators. He's terrified of the elevator. Shall we have them meet daily on the second floor of an office building only to depart alone into the pliant shape of their particular neuroses? Is it not a shape out of which, like the space between avoidance and terror, one might sculpt an uplifting conclusion, broad and directive as a hallway? Why, even now, I can see one of them standing there, moving slowly toward the stairs. I can't tell if it's her or if it's him. The problem is neither can you.

The Problem

He learns that a distant relative bred singing crickets in China. Funny, distance is always relative. For example, those telephone wires, those ones there, are both fifteen feet away and nearly five miles from here. And here's something else: of the four distinct cricket songs, my favorite is the copulatory one. The problem isn't putting things together. That's easy enough. The problem is prying them apart.

The Problem

Her lover tells her that his grandfather used to spit incessantly, each time excusing it as Christ's way of returning sight to the blind. The problem, after all, is not ours, but the way we see it.

The Problem

After a lengthy exposition, the comedian appears to have forgotten the punch line, which is rather unexpected, eliciting a round of laughter from the audience, and becoming thusly a kind of punch line. A tree can become a table. A table, a desk. A desk becomes a kind of bed if one is tired enough. One's drowsiness becomes a dream of endless stage lights. The audience erupts. The problem is with what?

The Problem

If she does it, then he certainly won't do it, disappointing them, although it's what we've expected all along. If we do it, she's sure to harbor some misgivings, and they'll feel slighted yet a little at ease, while he'll, no doubt, expect nothing less. If I do it, I plan on complete discretion, as I don't know how they'll react, nor how she'll take it, but he's sure to admonish me. If he does it, which I assume has already happened, I'll study my initial reaction until it blossoms into the kind of acceptance they expect of me, wearing it like a new shirt, one she's bound to comment on, never, in all these years, having seen me in it. The problem is the buttons seem to be on the wrong side.

Refresh. Refresh. Refresh.

Poems shouldn't make you wait for them to finish.
Like love, they should finish making you wait.

The Problem

A cricket keeps him up. A coworker puts him down. He's shaken by a death, rattled by an ex-lover, and put through the wringer by a needy friend. His boss walks all over him. His tennis partner tears him apart. He's propped up by his newfound money and thrown a curve by its subsequent loss. One could go on and on like this, wading in the misfortunate joy of language as though it were a public swimming pool, idiomatically chlorinated, yet so clear. Let's talk about the difference between a blackbird and a black bird. The materiality of language is a phrase poets like to throw around. The problem is it still hasn't landed anywhere.

The Problem

She receives monthly letters in broken English from
the child she sponsors, but has yet to respond. This is
the best thing I have to say about autobiography. It is
like photographing the back of a tourist photographing
his family in front of a famous landmark. Have you ever
cleaned someone else's mess in the bathroom because
you were afraid the next person in line would think
it your own? The circumstances are irrelevant. That's
the problem.

The Problem

I have seven quarters which I am unable to assemble into
a dollar. Together, they make almost two, but never one.
There I go, thinking of sex again. The birds in the trees are
allegorical. Any birds. Any trees. The problem is formal.
It takes the form of a washing machine. It takes exactly
one dollar.

The Problem

Two people perform a nearly 45-minute dialogue in which they discuss their respective careers, relationship troubles, dinner plans, and the particulars of a week's worth of unseasonable weather; small pockets of subdued laughter turn into feverous cackles as it dawns on the audience that this dialogue is comprised entirely of movie titles. It would be expected of the reader to now scan the page for proof, and perhaps come upon the following sentence: At a national writer's conference, a rather gregarious woman parades around in a t-shirt that reads *watch out or you'll end up in my novel.* Just as the two performers are oblivious to the audience, so the woman is to the reader, and I to the problem, which walks like a man into a bar before leaving Grand Central Station traveling north at precisely 11 a.m.

The Problem

On his medication, he is normal; off his medication he is
more himself. I like you just the way you are. The problem
is lyrical.

The Problem

Her latest biography is of the writer famous less for his novels than for the public admission that in order to clear his head before writing he maintains a daily practice of vigorous, erotic auto-asphyxiation. I admit this is a fiction. What form of the verb *to be* isn't? This is, in fact, the problem.

The Problem

The poster depicts a toy gun painted black and a real gun painted red. "It's not the one you think," it reads. The problem keeps changing color. It's not the one you think.

The Problem

In the distance, a little dot; now, an outline, a tiny shape that as we zoom in takes on that of a ship, an ocean liner. And there, on deck, a couple lounging in the sun. She's written a book about him and he's written a book about her and between these books there's an oceanic expanse. In the distance, a little dot; now, an outline, a tiny shape that as we zoom in takes on that of the problem.

The Dubtone

Imagine

being

prone

to bits

The Problem

Fresh out of art school, he lands a job painting cartoon ducks on the knobs of children's dressers. This, these ducks all day for a company whose owner is tyrannically overbearing, demanding in no uncertain terms that he up production to a near-impossible level. There's something about the phrase "no uncertain terms" that I'd like to explore. The problem is I'm not sure how to do so. It's the rabbit-duck dilemma par excellence. With a raised eyebrow, he turns them all evil. See how easy it is? All I do is mention a crown, and already it's like he's king of the rabbit kingdom. Now I remember, no uncertain terms are interchangeable.

The Problem

She has an idea for a film in which a woman making a sandwich talks about her trip to Sweden having been a disappointment. It takes her almost an hour to explain this. She wrings her hands while speaking. The problem is it also takes her (the other one) almost an hour to explain this.

The Problem

His little sister was as a young child obsessed with kites, which she would collect and marvel over, spreading them out on the living room table, but never, not even once, daring to fly them. As for me, when I was much younger, I flew a kite whose string I'd wound directly around my palm, a mistake the first gust of wind made terribly apparent. That's an interesting phrase—terribly apparent, something I could see myself marveling over. It's not cinematic, exactly, but there is a touch of color to it that suggests movement, a red speck or two in the distance; maybe they're kites. The problem is maybe they're not.

The Problem

The microphone is too sensitive, picking up the move-
ment of saliva in his mouth during the interview. He's
a famous writer, famous for his novelistic memoir, for
rendering truth with a literary flair. I'm not making this
up. The problem is ongoing. It sounds like he's masticat-
ing his answers. When he's finished speaking, the sound
continues.

The Problem

First, there were a lot of gods. Then there was one, but a lot of ones. Can I tell you that what I most admire about the arachnid is the mechanics of so many legs in motion? After a while, the problem adds up to something infinite. And then, then there's just us counting it.

Continental Realism

Immanuel, in the last snow of the first night
I feel perfectly calm. A violin doesn't play.

There is no one playing it. What is perfection?
Snow falling on the word *snowfall*. There

is no such thing. Immanuel, there is no such
thing there as there is no such thing.

The Problem

Because he's forgotten which toothbrush is his, the man squeezes a small amount of toothpaste onto his fingertip and applies it like so. We watch him do this, knowing that he is a stranger, that neither toothbrush belongs to him. Allow me to demonstrate. It is often difficult to tell a capital *I* from a lowercase *l*. The problem, of course, is not a case of mistaken identity. By way of commentary I offer only that this film lasts for hours, and we're restless and hungry. The problem is I mean both of us.

The Problem

after Donna Stonecipher

An Asian man speaking with a Jamaican accent places an order for spaghetti at a Greek restaurant in downtown Prague. There is no problem.

The Problem

One juror finds another's book about the scandalous trial in the remainder bin. This could be the beginning of a movie. Why didn't I think of that? One juror finds another's book about the scandalous trial in the remainder bin. See how time in this sentence is different? The problem is this could also be the beginning of a movie.

The Problem

The bus driver's daily walk to work takes him under an overpass where above roosts a flight of pigeons. Every morning, she rides the bus to work and reads again the large poster inside: "Please respect your bus driver. They are working hard to do their job." For him, the problem is clear. For her, it's the possibility that the job being done is not that of driving a bus. For me, it's that a flight of pigeons sounds awkwardly like an error. You can hear it, can't you? That faint humming?

The Problem

He kissed his third cousin once, in the rain, under a canopy of branches and kudzu, on a Wednesday afternoon. Incidentally, today is also Wednesday. I like to think of it as the third day of the week. The problem is it's the fourth.

The Problem

A painting of a photograph based on a short film about a piece of music commemorating the anniversary of a famous novel's publication is still a painting. A photograph based on a short film about a piece of music commemorating the anniversary of a famous novel's publication is still a photograph. A short film about a piece of music commemorating the anniversary of a famous novel's publication is still a short film. A piece of music commemorating the anniversary of a famous novel's publication is still a piece of music. The problem is the anniversary of a famous novel's publication is just an anniversary.

The New Brutalism

René, it is not winter in the ruined boat
Pieces of a man hung from the bridge
René, the truth is not important
The shadow of two gnats on a page
Likewise the head is easily removed from the body

The Problem

I interview a nonfiction writer who desires above all else to sustain in her work an unfaltering clarity. Here's a question: at what age is it no longer appropriate to attach a leash to one's child? A succession of unrelated events might imply a story, but that's just your doing. I mean this with all the sincerity I can muster. This really happened. The problem is so did that.

The Problem

The problem is how that ship got inside the bottle. No, the problem is that the line "How that ship got inside the bottle" appears on page 56 of *The Collected Poems of Philip Whalen*, in a poem he wrote in 1956, and now also appears here, in the 56th problem, which is not a problem at all, but a coincidence, which makes this, of course, a problem.

The Problem

She publishes in a national magazine an essay detailing the ubiquitous and often thinly-veiled racism of her newly adopted neighborhood. The essay is met with immediate rebuke. The rebuke matures into scorn, the scorn into threat, and the immediacy into her fear of the neighbors figuring out which of the local faces might belong to her. Because hers is uncommon, she's now giving false names in restaurants and coffee shops. Can an essay on the history of nonfiction pass as a nonfiction article on the history of the essay? Can I write a poem in prose about real events as they've been reported to me without aestheticizing those involved? Is a literary genre also a social construct? She waits, but no one calls her name. A name is called, but no one answers. The problem is not that pseudonyms are too easy to forget, but that we fictionalize the privilege of forgetting.

The Problem

The entry for *fetus* in the encyclopedia given to her by her mother reads, simply: *see embryo*. Because there is no entry for *embryo*, the problem refuses further development. It just sits there expectantly, sort of moving, but not really. Well, maybe a little.

The Problem

For weeks a sharp pain so troubles him while chewing that
he no longer uses one side of his mouth, the side on which
the dentist, when he does finally visit, is unable to find
anything out of the ordinary. Here, I could quote Yeats.
For example, "Personality is born out of pain." My friend
Richard once leveled the following complaint against me:
"Noah thinks that bar is too common." Here, I could quote
Eliot. For example, "The progress of an artist is a continual
self-sacrifice, a continual extinction of personality." It is of-
ten difficult to tell the difference between the common and
the ordinary. Pain, on the other hand, is always personal.
The problem is I'm the one troubled by quotation.

The Problem

I like to think about Kierkegaard. Hey, it looks like spell-check isn't even bothered by that—Kierkegaard without a red wavy line! Kierkegaard in a word document. The word Kierkegaard. Red wavy lines under everything but Kierkegaard. We aren't so boring after all! For example, I also like to think about the three kinds of apostrophe—how the first adds something; the next takes it away; and the final one, my favorite, just impassionedly points. The problem is it does this with a circle.

An Old Branch Of Meter
On The Half-Dead Tree

abstract as a mirror to an antelope

as a piece of the pinkish day

to an airplane cutting it overhead

a miniature symphony

that may be a watercolor

in the gears of the silverfish

in the photograph of a misshapen riverbed

in the language of musical notation

in charcoal and chalk on paper

glass and a mouth underneath

The Problem

He's uninterested in the events within her novel but in awe of the intricate filigree with which she ornaments them. It takes a few thousand words for someone to approach the throne. It's taken me seven cigarettes to get through the third sentence. Is the idling engine of an unseen insect within earshot imageless? Is this an unrelated question? I think I hear a perfectly reasonable subject, says the king. The problem is no one's talking.

The Problem

If she moves her pawn, his queen might take her rook, but she'll be able to bring her knight into play. If he moves his king, she'll know he's planning to corner her with both bishops. I have a plan to type out verbatim a famous novel, rearrange in reverse order its sentences, and publish it as my own book. That this has nothing to do with chess is the problem.

The Problem

She's made a point of hanging a small photograph of an
eighteenth-century clipper ship in the bathroom of each of
the now seven apartments in which she's lived. If you look
closely, you can barely make out two men waving from
the deck; one, a head taller than the other. Is that a piano
I hear coming from several houses down? A light snow
has settled on the landing. The problem is which landing.

The Problem

All this talk about problems in the singular, about their uselessness and futility, about our utter inability to work them out, suggests to the average, engaged reader a sort of rarified, refined, even ostentatious approach to our lives as we live them. Such problems are not real problems. Such sentences are simply statements. As against this, an actual problem must be something utilitarian, servile, unrefined, obsequious, humble. It must be an absolute entry point for our individual problems to open to an equally absolute plurality. It must be the opposite of a statement, but one that staunchly refuses ossification into the rigidity of a question. The interrogative mode in which we attempt to account for our place in the world is so much fodder for flimsy, mutable, and unending answers. This is the problem, or, more poignantly, this *are* the problem.

Acknowledgments

Portions of this manuscript previously appeared in the following journals: *200012*, *6x6*, *Aufgabe*, *Colorado Review*, *Fence*, *Lana Turner: A Journal of Poetry and Opinion*, *Peacock Online Review*, *Poor Claudia*, *THEthe Poetry*, Vlak (Czech Republic), and *Whiskey Island*. Portions of this work appeared in the exhibition *Verse, Stripped: A Poetry Comics Exhibition* at the Poetry Foundation in Chicago, IL and in the chapbook *Fifteen Problems* from Above/Ground Press. These problems were encountered mostly in Brooklyn, NY, in the summer of 2010, lingering on in Denver, CO, until about February of 2011.

NOAH ELI GORDON is the author of several books, including *The Word* Kingdom *in the Word Kingdom* (Brooklyn Arts Press, 2015) and *Novel Pictorial Noise*, which was selected by John Ashbery for the National Poetry Series and subsequently chosen for the San Francisco State Poetry Center Book Award. He teaches in the MFA Program for Creative Writing at the University of Colorado Boulder, where he currently directs Subito Press.